TRADING MINDFULLY

The Psychological Guide for Finding Consistency in an Irrational Environment

Copyright © 2019 Nick Schmidt

All rights reserved.

CONTENTS

About This Book 1

Introduction 4

Chapter 1 8

   THE MARKET RUNS ON EMOTION 8

      How Emotion Fuels the Stock Market 9

      How Fear Destroys the Stock Market 11

      The Power of Greed and Optimism 12

Chapter 2 17

   THE PSYCHOLOGY OF TRADING 17

      Wins and Losses 18

      How Winning Affects The Mind 21

      Psychological Response to Loss 22

      Take a Different Stance 25

      Avoid Mental Bias 26

Chapter 3 32

   BASIC BRAIN ANATOMY 32

      The Trading Brain 33

      Finding Your Balance 36

      Train Your Brain to Be the Expert 37

      Novices 38

      Experts 39

      Training 40

Chapter 4 41

TRADING REQUIRES CALCULATED RISKS 41
Determine Your Trading Size 42
Drawdowns, Frequencies and Trading Style 43

Chapter 5 47
TRADING IN PROBABILITIES 47
Avoid the Flaws of Instinctual Trading 48

Chapter 6 51
CONSTRUCTIVE SELF-DEVELOPMENT 51
What Kind of Trader Are You? 51
A Word on Consistency 53
A Confident Outlook 54
Focus on the Process 55
Developing Resilience 56

Chapter 7 58
STRESS MANAGEMENT TO EXERT CONTROL 58
Practice Meditation 61
Positive Thought Reframing 63
Restructure Time and Activities 64
Micro-breaks and Mini-vacations 65
Create Your Own Stock Strategy 68
A Very Basic Look at Stock Market Advice 69
Choose Your Overall Goal Wisely 70

Chapter 8 72
MEDITATION AND MINDFUL TRADING 72
What is Mindful Meditation? 75
Practice Mindful Trading 76

    A Basic Form of Mindfulness 78

    Tips to Get Started with Mindful Practice 80

Chapter 9 83

    TEN TIPS TO GET YOU STARTED TOWARDS TRADING CORRECTLY 83

        1.   Educate Yourself or Find an Educated Helper 84

        2.   Figure out Your Ultimate Goals 85

        3.   Stick to a Plan and Rules That Makes Sense 87

        4.   Maintain Individuality in the Face of Herd Mentality 88

        5.   Protect Yourself From 'Ooh, Something Shiny!' Decisions 89

        6.   Think and Research Before You Act 90

        7.   Take Time to Imagine "Winning" 91

        8.   Stop Analysis Paralysis 92

        9.   Cultivate Smart Responses to Loss 93

        10. Keep Long-term Records and Journals 95

Chapter 10 96

    HANDLING A TRADE DRAWDOWN 96

        1.   Accept That There is No Way to Avoid These Risks 98

        2.   Change Your Perspective 99

        3.   Avoid Increasing Your Position Size 100

        4.   Avoid Making Adjustments to Your Trading Method 101

        5.   Measure Your Drawdowns 101

        6.   Think About the Long-Term Goal 102

        7.   Analyze the Past 102

        8.   Learn to Step Away from the Screen 103

Conclusion 105

About This Book

If you are an avid trader, this book provides a set formula for you to follow. It does not tell you which stocks to buy, when to sell, or how much money to risk on any investment. Instead, it reveals the unpleasant truths that keep the unprofitable rate hovering around 95%. Ultimately, your decision to succeed depends on your ability to manage your emotions and expectations in an environment that is uncomfortable.

Everything you need to succeed, other than data and the essential how-to information, comes from your mind. My goal is to help you discover these things, manage your attitudes and expectations, and make intelligent decisions while you continue or start your trading career.

The stock market offers a wealth of opportunity. It did not

always seem like that. If you ask other people in your life, you will find a lot of negative opinions about this mysterious world. Some people believe that stocks are the ultimate wealth-building machine, while others warn against putting any money on the line and are incredibly averse to risk. The majority of these recommendations come from past experiences and emotional opinions, sometimes formed without any evidence to support these claims.

The financial services industry grows yearly. Companies and individuals who specialize in helping other people invest exist to make money, just like any other business. It is in their best interest to keep you confused and unsure about the entire process. After all, if you felt confident in your knowledge and skills, you would not need to pay their fees to take care of things for you.

Fund managers and active traders are always seeking information that will broaden their horizon on trading. The drive to expand their abilities and become consistently profitable is there. However, there is a hard time sifting through all of the information given to us. Whether it is a trading service on Twitter or the talking heads on the TV, there are so many opinions thrown around and secret strategies being sold that you don't know what to believe.

The stock market will exist forever or at least for as long as the world's financial systems continue to operate in the usual manner. Whether you directly invest or not, it has something to do with finance all around the globe. Since it is such an intrinsic part of how things operate, why not learn to use it for your gain, rather than avoid it like so many do?

Introduction

An individual's impression of the stock market highly depends on the level of knowledge and interaction that they have with it. Some may conjure up images of people in suits waving their hands, staring upward at monitors with wide eyes on the stock exchange floor. Others may view the market as something mysterious that helps fund their 401(k) retirement accounts. Whether you are distanced from it due to lack of understanding, investment ability, or you are intricately involved with its day-to-day fluctuations, more goes into the relationship than you think.

On the surface, the idea of the stock market seems simple. Industries prosper, companies' profit, and stocks go up. However, a closer look reveals that the process is confusing and chaotic. Unfathomable things that can destroy a person's financial future or send it soaring to new lofty heights can occur in a split second.

A lot can happen between the opening & closing bells. Even when we sleep, more can happen overnight. During those dark hours, business operations are in full force and will affect everyone the following day. For active traders, who are our focus here, you can make decisions that can affect your future entirely with just a laptop or your cell phone. We are at liberty of doing this at home, at work, on vacation, on the way to a shopping mall, or even on the bus. You make the decisions and must take responsibility for exactly what happens to your money.

Nothing can stop you from wielding this ultimate power. It's incredibly exciting and even a bit overwhelming. A few simple taps and swipes can mean the difference between a comfortable retirement and long-term struggles. You are your boss, and nothing is holding you back - *except yourself.*

It is commonly said that about 95% of traders don't make money from the market. However, this evaluation is not a fact. Research shows that less than 5% of traders make money in the market. [i] If the stock market is made up of endless opportunities every day, and everyone has access to a wide array of tools on their computers, why does the overwhelming majority lose money?

The stock market is a 'structure-less,' free-flowing entity that has absolutely no rules. Many people are used to formats and following guidelines. You won't find that in the stock market, rules must be self-made and adhered to, and this requires serious discipline. For such a massive potential of earning power, such a small number of profitable traders seems almost ridiculous.

- Why do so many people miss out on the opportunities or misjudge the appropriate times to buy and sell?
- Why do people get involved if they are so likely to lose money?

A possible reason is that people like to gamble, and the stock market can act as a giant casino for many. We will dive into that later in the book. More than anything else, the success comes down to your psychology as it relates to the system.

You may want a set list of rules to follow or the ultimate system guaranteed to make you money in the market, but it does not exist. Why? Every trader approaches the market with their own mental attitudes and behaviors that affect everything from stock choices to how they react when something goes wrong.

These emotions are at the heart of the market. The market runs on emotions. From buying and selling, everyone is trying to be right but what nobody talks about is how hard it is to see your money increase or decrease by a significant amount and the next step to take.

What is the next step? That is different for everybody, their circumstances, and time frame. What isn't unique is the emotional imbalances that we all face internally in the face of watching our hard-earned money fluctuate. Being a successful trader has absolutely nothing to do with your IQ but everything to do with your EQ (Emotional Intelligence).

Chapter 1

THE MARKET RUNS ON EMOTION

Only around 5% of the people who invest in the stock market make any considerable amount of money. We tend to wonder, what are these few individuals doing differently? While some earn more because they invest more, others seem to get lucky with purchase and sale timing. The truth is that most of them have no discernible difference than the other 95% that fails to make profits. They have no intrinsic benefits that increase the possibility of them making money.

If you want to join those top investors, the first thing to understand is that *you are not missing out on some super-secret method or merely lacking in intelligence or skill*. What you require is the EQ and the discipline to prosper in a continually fluctuating environment.

How Emotion Fuels the Stock Market

If your optimism and loss aversion can affect your investment success levels, it stands to reason that the same psychological effects in the whole population of investors can have much more significant effects on the overall market itself.

A well-known belief about the stock market is that, instead of money, the emotions of greed and fear fuel it.

However, research studies[ii] have also confirmed this theory; they have connected the ups and downs we witness in the market as an occurrence resulting from the emotional excitement most investors feel.

Some researchers from UC Berkeley using 495 participants further determined the diverse emotional states[iii] we all feel when trading. From their deductions, the different kinds of emotional ups and downs we feel are some of the principal driving forces in the market[iv].

Many average investors underestimate the impacts of

emotions. Collectively, the feelings not only affect our decisions individually but can make the value of any stock rise or crash. It can cause dramatic swings in the market and individual stock valuations[v].

Well-known businessman and investor Warren Buffett once said, "I will tell you how to become rich. Close the doors. Be fearful when others are greedy and greedy when others are fearful."[vi]

The diversion from what the rest of the market is doing can lead to success because you are in control of your emotional response.

Human emotions are fundamental in every decision-making process. Those gut feelings as we all acknowledge help us assess situations that can benefit or hurt us. So, it influences our tendencies or readiness to act. Diverse emotions have peculiar actions[vii] they can cause us to take. For example, the same fear that can cause us to flee in a survival situation can also cause investors to pull out, in some cases, irrationally from the stock market, which leads to a downturn.

So, when you learn to master it, you will see the transformations in the daily decisions you make.

How Fear Destroys the Stock Market

As the stock market numbers fall, people get scared. The excitements, euphoria, or thrill, you feel when your investments become more valuable disappears faster the moment they begin to fall. This volatility of emotion affects you more than if the market stayed relatively stable with smaller fluctuations.

Stock market crashes occur when the fear overtakes any objective understanding of what is going on or what people should do to protect their interests. According to a 2010 study[viii], the fear of losing can make some investors reject opportunities that would have been profitable.

According to that study, the actions we take as a result of this fear comes from the *amygdala*, which is the almond-shaped center in the brain, responsible for controlling fear and other acute emotions. The fears we usually associate with trading includes the **fear of missing out, fear of letting profit become a loss, fear of taking losses, and the fear of not being right**[ix]. Sometimes this fear can be beneficial, other times; it can lead us towards making the wrong decisions.

Of course, it is terrifying to see your retirement fund or investment portfolio suddenly drop in value. Therefore, we must exert the type of emotional control this book promotes. How do you overcome the vulnerability and loss aversion, so that you can recognize that Warren Buffett's quote is the right way forward?

The Power of Greed and Optimism

Most people view greed as a negative thing. You may associate it with always wanting more, coveting material possessions, or focusing on money above all else. While insatiability can cause problems if you draw your motivation only by financial gain, that is also the main point of investing in the stock market. Greed and fear, which appears to be two opposing emotional states, are foundational factors that increase the volatility and unpredictability of the stock market. So, in general, making sure none of your emotions or responses to market fluctuations gets too extreme is the key to long-term success.

Optimism, on the other hand, has a favorable impression. Although it comes down to the same outcome, when speaking about Wall Street investments – more money – the emotional impact of the word is different from the one you get when you think of greed.

Greed causes people to purchase stocks, even when the statistics and stock prices do not indicate you should. According to research[x], it results in a chemical rush that causes us to set aside self-control and common sense while making decisions. This is a decision fueled by emotion rather than practicality or intellect. When it comes to investing, you can regard optimism as the light and fluffy form of greed. If you become so emotionally sure that the prices will rise despite indications of the opposite, you end up in as much difficulty as you would if a more negative emotion-fueled your decision.

In the past 100 years, the stock market has risen and fallen so many times. It has made millionaires and destroyed dreams and will continue to do so far into the future. If you look at statistical evidence for the biggest crashes or booms, you will find that waves of emotion such as fear and greed either caused or exacerbated the highs and lows on the charts.

Any chart of a stock market crash looks virtually the same. Of course, the average value of the S&P 500 and other measurements decrease. However, the actual daily or monthly level jumps up and down considerably in a very volatile way.[xi]

This clearly shows the swing of fear and greed throughout the entire investing population. If things start going back up, people react, and whatever emotion fuels their trading decisions increases exponentially throughout the market. In essence, these two emotions create market volatility.

The entire cycle of stock market-focused emotion includes:[xii]

- Optimism, excitement, and euphoria as the prices and your investment increases
- Denial, fear, and panic as the market begins to fall
- Depression, relief, and optimism again as the cycle begins anew

How do you stop this seemingly natural process from affecting your investment strategy? Can you train your mind to overcome the fear response when your stock purchases begin to struggle? Can you avoid being swept along in the greed and optimism of a market that seems like the right choice at the time?

The answers to these questions ultimately depend on your ability to temper emotion with intellect. *This does not mean you must cultivate an attitude of hard, unfeeling stoicism.*

What it means is that you need to understand how emotion transforms your trading in the end. Emotions are essential in decision-making and vital to your trading decisions. They are the reasons we have preferences and predispositions to act in a particular manner.

There is even a myth that you can trade without emotions[xiii]. You must realize that this myth is baseless and impossible. Emotions are okay as long as you learn how to control them. In reality, they can add quality to the decisions we make. Often enough, some studies have shown that without emotions, we can also cause bad choices leading to more chaotic outcomes. According to Hans Pinter[xiv], emotions are an integral part of rational decision making.

It isn't the emotions that cause problems for the trader, but the sudden irrational and overwhelming feels that it offers them. Successful traders not only accept their feelings but find ways always to ensure they don't base their decisions solely on them. They have realized that it's all about how they apply those thoughts and emotions. They have also recognized the distinct mental boundaries we all have, which can distort the information before us and influence the decisions we make, leading to predictable errors in trading. Once you recognize how emotion feeds into the entire trading world, you become better equipped to override your natural inclinations and follow the advice of one of the most successful investors in the world and realize your financial success over time.

Chapter 2

THE PSYCHOLOGY OF TRADING

The caricature of a stock market success story includes an expensive suit, fast-talk, eyes on the prize, and a certain measure of fearless ego. This is not the type of attitude you need to earn money on your investments. It's not also about celebrating trades that pool in money and ignoring trades that lose money. It is about controlling the two primary emotions that influences trading – fear and greed[xv]. You must develop a mindset that allows you to overcome internal battles that stop you from reaching your full potential.

Stock trading is tough, and you need to understand the psychology behind the decisions to both succeed and do so without succumbing to stress. It is this type of understanding that will allow you to see how the same cycles and processes occur over and over again. If you do this, you will learn how to use them effectively to grow wealth. Ponder on these words;

"The four most dangerous words in investing are this time it's different." – Sir John Templeton

You must realize that the same things happen over and over again. Human nature, emotions, and actions don't change. The patterns and decisions all happen repeatedly. You have to embrace that fact so you can actively look for those patterns and contain your emotions. Even when we look at our different national, cultural, and social backgrounds, we all make the same basic mistakes. We will always have the same psychological responses.

Wins and Losses

Look at these psychological scenarios first assessed by Brett Steenbarger[xvi]:

Scene 1:

A student wishes to pass a final exam to complete a specific year in school. He has already written several exams, but they bordered between passing and failing, and the course grade entirely rides on the final. The big test is approaching, so the student finds himself worried about the test, mainly because he missed some questions in the practice exams. Because of this worry, his sleep is affected, and soon, he becomes worried that fatigue may affect his performance. By the time he needs to take the final exam, he is nervous, tired, and misses many questions because he is busy second-guessing the right answers.

Scene 2:

A person needs to give a presentation which would be a turning point in her career but has before now been uncomfortable with public speaking. The results from this presentation will be the difference between landing a major client or losing a client to a competitor. During the presentation, she discovers that some of the participants she is trying to woo were not attentive. Because of what she noticed, she became anxious and desperately tried to boost up the presentation. Due to the rise in her anxiety level, she became flustered, and the presentation ended on a stuttered note.

Scene 3:

A basketball player has been the team's leading scorer, but

at the start of a game, misses his first five shots. This happens because the opposing team is double-teaming him, and so he is facing challenges finding ways to get to the basket. He begins taking matters into his hands and decides to penetrate the opposing defense to draw fouls. Instead, he gets two quick charging calls and so becomes fearful that he might be taken out of the game. Because of this fear, he tries to get his shot by moving out of the perimeter, and when it doesn't fall, he stops looking and continues making errant passes.

Scene 4:

A trader has some winning in a row and is feeling confident. So, he decides to enhance the size and apply his hot streak. Initially, there are successes in his favor, but soon it reverses, and the large orders push the market lower. When he evaluates his position, he realized that he had lost all the profit from previous trades. He becomes determined to get back what he has lost and so, reenters the market. This time he faces a second wave of selling. Because he encountered challenges the first time, he begins second-guessing his decisions and so trades with a reduced size. At the close of the market, he is down on the day and the week and feels depressed about allowing his overconfidence to overshadow his decisions.

Many of these patterns exist all around the world. Scene 1, scene 2, and scene 3 may not directly express the market, but it sheds insights on how particular habits if allowed, can lead to ruin.

How Winning Affects The Mind

People like to win. This obvious statement extends to everything from a pickup game of basketball to the success of a long-term relationship to the stock market. With something as important as investing money, winning comes with an even more forceful response. As the stock market provides the opportunity to either win or lose every day, it makes sense that emotions play a considerable part in the entire investment process.

Although many people may consider that winning at anything feels good because it is a positive outcome, there are actual physiological responses to it. Researchers have studied it more in the realm of sports and games and have found that making a lot of money through great investments gives the same outcome. Both men and women were shown to get a boost of testosterone when they won various competitions.[xvii] In turn, dopamine levels rise.

What does this have to do with your behavior in the stock market?

Testosterone elevation causes feelings of power and capability across the board. Dopamine is one of those "feel-good" chemicals created in your brain. If you make a smart trade and earn money, you will automatically feel more likely to win again. This will give you a boost that may override any fear or uncertainty about making the next trade. On the surface, this sounds quite positive. After all, you need to keep investing if you want to keep getting a positive return. However, this natural body process triggered by a win can lead you to make hasty decisions in a quest to repeat the physiological response. Your natural response to success needs to balance with your sense of control.

It is known across the industry, for many traders, the most significant loss will come right after the biggest wins, and this is why. This is why luck runs out in the market; any lucky gains will often be erased by undisciplined actions that are propelled by our elevated hormones.

Psychological Response to Loss
If you lose a game or money in the stock market, the exact

opposite physiological response occurs. You have lower levels of testosterone, which saps the feeling of confidence and power, and your dopamine does not trigger in the same way. Everyone knows they feel bad when they lose. The most important thing to remember is that you do not have to let that emotional response inform future action.

Interestingly enough, the concept of loss aversion does not seem to affect stock market investors as much as many people think.[xviii] Loss aversion is the desire to avoid losing. The opposite is the drive to pursue a win. As mentioned above, no one wants to lose. You automatically feel better when you win. This balance of forces working on your psychological and emotional self encourages you to take specific actions in the stock market.

However, a study in the *Journal of Consumer Psychology* showed that people are more likely to take a chance to increase the possibility of winning than they are to avoid any risk due to the fear of losing.[xix] Again, every individual has their comfort level with risk, attitudes toward loss aversion, and physiological response to both winning and losing.

Your job as a trader is to work through or around emotional

responses to make the smartest decisions about investments. Fear and drastic enthusiasm can both lead you to bad or hasty decisions that have significant effects on your overall investment portfolio. This is what makes the 95% earn very little or lose. This is also what fueled some of the most volatile changes in the market throughout history.

"If you are pained by any external thing, it is not this thing that disturbs you, but your own judgment about it. And it is in your power to wipe out this judgment now." - *Marcus Aurelius, Meditations*

If you take a loss and feel any pain, it is because of your false expectations. You must look internally and realize that the issue of this problem arises from the self. You probably expected it to be a winner when you put on the trade instead of truly accepting that every trade has a random outcome. You are playing a game of probabilities; there are no certainties. When you place a trade, you must expect that it may come back and hit your stop loss. When you expect a random outcome and truly accept that there is no certainty, you begin to form a healthier relationship with your losses, and this is one of the first steps to becoming a consistently profitable trader.

Take a Different Stance

Cultivate the habit of avoiding the temptation of seeing losing trades as 'bad' and profitable trades as 'good.' Avoid equating loss to failure, no matter how big or small that loss is. Many traders cannot even accept a small loss that doesn't hurt their capital or trading account. They hold on to such behavior because they see losses and failure as the same thing. So, when they avoid losing at all cost, they might either close their winning trades too soon or hang on to losing trades for too long.

As stated earlier, you are playing a game of probabilities. So, although we expect winnings all the time, it can go both ways. Avoid sticking to the mindset that you can avoid losing trades *at all cost*. With such a mindset, there would be a higher risk of failing. To beat the market, you must be more conscious of the biases that can lead to irrational choices and conclusions. You must keep reminding yourself about these biases because it is only with a keen awareness that you can overcome them and keep your mind focused on the right things. As Gary Dayton[xx] would be quick to point out, these are mental blind spots or the limitations in cognitive reasoning. These psychological biases are efficient for our daily lives, but in trading, they have been found to lead to poor judgments.

Avoid Mental Bias

1. The Representativeness Heuristic

In this case, we simplify trading tasks by looking for a shortcut to solve the problem. These shorten the mental load and leads to faster decision-making. So, instead of trying to make sense of complex data, we look for a simple approach that should produce an okay result. Many of us use heuristics in our daily decision making. Sometimes, it works out fine, other times, it can result in more disaster. Heuristics have helped a lot of us manage the world more efficiently. But when used in trading, it leads to more errors in judgment. Taking such a simplified logical path in a condition of uncertainty, risks, or probabilities can bring about poor outcomes and significant errors.

2. The Recency Effect

In this case, we base our deductions on present events instead of looking at the data over time. This happens because the current event is much more memorable than what occurred earlier. By lending weight to the most recent events, we base our expectations of the market on them. There are lots of ways these events can occur. Some traders might even base their predictions of how the market will unfold on those recent events alone. Bear in mind that this can happen in both winning and losing trades.

We must retain the mindset that the current events we see cannot influence the activities of the future. This effect can make us forget about validating background data. It usually happens when we have a few winnings in a row. We begin to think that we are on a hot streak where our abilities, skills, or intuition have so improved that we are interpreting the market better than everyone else. When we have this bias, we have higher tendencies of committing trading errors such as entering marginally qualified trades, increasing position size, or even overtrading.

It's also possible to base deductions on recent events when our trades have poor recent performances. In this case, it can lead us to withdraw from a market because we want to cut our losses. It can also lead to the opposite, where we double the position size or take on additional trades we had no plans for because we want to recover what has been lost. Whether you were on a winning or losing streak, basing decisions on recent events can lead to erratic trading behaviors which can make us commit trading errors.

3. Hindsight Bias

This kind of bias refers to the *"I knew it all along effect."* In this case, we act as if we have, in some way, had a complete understanding of the future.

The Hindsight bias occurs in three levels: the first is the belief that the outcome was specific and that it had to happen; the second comes from flawed memories of an earlier event where it felt as though we made that prediction, which, in reality, we did not.

The third is having the belief that we can know what's ahead of time. Hindsight bias often leads to selecting particular information from the miles of data before us, to validate the fact that we *know* what's going to happen next. Like the representative heuristics, we look for a simple solution, but in this case, a solution based on what we feel *"we knew all along."*

There are many consequences of the hindsight bias. One of them is the feeling of regret we often have after losses. We begin to feel we should have seen that coming or *"thought of that"* or *"done that."* With such feelings, many traders have been tempted into taking up a marginal trade to try and make up for those feelings of regret.

Another consequence of hindsight bias is that it prevents us from learning the real reasons why the market or our trading went in a different direction. We might feel that because *we knew all along,* why do we waste the efforts of trying to examine what was obvious? With such false convictions, we may even underestimate our strengths as traders, and when a similar pattern emerges in the future, we might be misinformed and unprepared to take on the approach for that trade.

4. The Endowment Effect[xxi]

In this case, the trader may hold on to a losing position rather than exit the trade. This is the opposite of cutting a winning trade short. When we feel we own something, we ascribe a perceived value or become emotionally attached to it. This is commonly seen when someone is constantly doing research in favor of their position. They are valuing that position more than other opportunities and looking to continually validate it. In the face of this bias, the only way out is objective thinking. It is a common saying "Do not marry your stocks" and this is why. You must form a healthy relationship with your positions and be able to swiftly make decisions regarding them without feeling any emotional pushback.

5. Base Rate Neglect[xxii]

This is the tendency to overlook trade probabilities, sometimes in favor of recent events, and at other times, in support of salient features or different improbable reasoning. So, just like the recency effect, the trader may ignore the past and focus on the recent without considering that the past events may also occur. For instance, an investor might base deductions on how a company may outperform its competitor by only looking at its recent earnings report rather than the proven records and consistent earnings over time[xxiii]. If you are basing your assumptions on only the information which you choose to include than you are not observing and evaluating the full data available.

We all have biases, and many other biases exist. What makes the difference is our awareness of them. It is effortless to be controlled by our cognitive as well as emotional biases. This is even higher when we are not aware that we are making them. In everyday life, they can go unnoticed and are okay. But when trading, only keen awareness can help us avoid making those mistakes. Understand the way your mind works; assess your emotional and cognitive blind spots. Even an inexperienced trader can keep the errors down with diligent awareness. *Always remember that most of these biases emerge from our abilities to seek shortcuts.* Pay attention to overall market conditions and ask yourself disconfirming questions or conduct alternative trade analysis.

With keen awareness, we can realize when these biases are becoming obstacles to our logical reasoning. Lastly, strive towards developing your expertise. By mastering the skills, technical analysis, and ability to read markets objectively, it will be easier to avoid judgmental errors.

Chapter 3

BASIC BRAIN ANATOMY

Our thinking and emotions are two primary aspects of our being that originate from the brain. The brain is the most potent structure known in the universe. It is the most complex mass and a self-organizing system of systems[xxiv]. It relies on the electrochemical impulses passing through it. These electrochemical impulses come from the 100 billion nerve cells in the body. It is within the brain that the functions of learning and memory occur by the reorganizations and strength of the neurons and synapses.

Your brain commands the entire process of trading, whether you like it or not. It's the reason you can see patterns, calculate risks, or execute trades. It is also in charge of how you first developed the idea to trade or the trading plan and the strategies you created.

All aspects of trading come from the processes in this unique organ. Whether you are a novice or expert, you must learn to use it. You must realize how important the brain is for decision making. It is the awareness and applications of the brain that differentiates the novice trader from the expert. To understand how experienced traders can limit their losses, we must assess the significant processes the brain undergoes each time we apply logical reasoning or intuition.

The Trading Brain

Generally, there are two aspects of the brain[xxv]. The right and left side of the brain have different functions, and the balance between these two areas is different in each of us. The left side (neocortex) of the brain is responsible for the analytical, logical, and practical deductions we make daily.

The right side (limbic cortex) of the brain is responsible for our creativity, intuition, and emotions. The right side of the brain can be sometimes called the reflexive, emotional, or primitive section of the brain. Both the limbic cortex and neocortex have their purposes, and we must find some balance between them.

You must realize that each one of us has different ratios for the use of each section of the brain. The two areas of the brain communicate consistently and are interpreting those impulses received on both sides of the brain. Therefore, there is a constant battle between both areas because there are times their deductions agree, and at other times they conflict. Depending on how you use them, there are lots of advantages and off course drawbacks.

For instance, when you have substantial left-brain advantages, you might function with a lot of practicality and discipline. On the other hand, when you have stronger tendencies of using the right part of the brain, you can lean towards using your intuition for trading. On the first instance, it's easy to see the left brain's benefits as better than those of the right side, but this is false information.

When you are predominantly 'left-brained,' you might become too rigid in your approach. You might end up overthinking, whereas there are times the market requires that you make swift decisions. On the other hand, if you are predominantly 'right-brained,' you may rely too much on your intuition which can be a severe disaster even when you have a splendid idea about the direction of the market. So, both areas have their unique benefits and drawbacks.

In reality, we all lean towards one side; no one can safely stay in the middle[xxvi]. If it were possible to stay in the middle, we might get a lot of confusing signals which means that our gut might be saying something else while our methodical approach leans towards another. If we picked to follow our gut and it leads to a win, we might abandon our trading plan for that which seems to look good. If we also decide to follow the systematic approach and it wins, we might be confused about our gut feelings as well.

Such confused states can make it challenging to overcome biases leading to a lot of judgmental errors. These can lead to a lot of problems in the future because we might begin to deviate from that carefully laid out plan that will bring better results in the future.

Moreover, you should also be aware that the brain uses memories to recognize, create, and recreate patterns. The brain uses those patterns to make decisions, engage ineffective behaviors, and solve problems. However, you must understand that the decisions come before the behavior. Therefore, whenever we execute trades, we are only performing the result of a circuit of the processes that had happened in the brain.

Finding Your Balance

As said earlier, we all have a different use of both sections of our brains. Trying to use equal portions of both is disastrous; on the other hand, becoming too methodical when you lean towards the creative side of your brain can be dangerous. The only right way for you is to find your natural disposition. Where does your right brain/left brain balance lie? There you will find the powerful tool to become successful.

In a broader sense, leaning towards your capabilities and efficiencies can be explained using positive psychology. Positive psychology is an attempt to base your decisions from creativity, spirituality, productive work, relationships, contentment, health, and much more. In the simplest terms, it denotes that we all have capacities and competencies for life fulfillment. According to Brett N. Steenbarger[xxvii], as derived from this branch of psychology, *we fall short not because of our weaknesses but because we underestimate our strengths.*

So, you must incorporate your greatest assets into every critical decision you make. It should influence your trading plan and the way you trade. Finding your balance between both areas of your brain will increase your self-awareness and help you make the best decisions.

Train Your Brain to Be the Expert

Some time ago, I came across a funny but accurate article by David Floyd. In this simple post; he talked about a study by the *Harvard University,* on the views of the brain while trading and taking cocaine to be very similar. He stated that the euphoria witnessed in the brain when those stocks are climbing in our favor is the same sensations experienced by addicts.

According to this paper, it is because of these activations in particular regions of the brain that can result in adverse decisions later, if we let those irrational biases creep in. Jason Zwei in his book, *Your Money and Your Brain*[xxviii], similarly stated the same deductions.

He further added that we process financial losses in the same areas where the brain processes response to mortal danger. Therefore, it is the awareness of how the brain works that will help you avoid following the psychological reactions of danger or euphoria when making your trading decisions. To further explain what happens in our brain, let us look at the brain of the expert and the novice trader.

Novices

For the novice or poorly trained trader, the intuitive part of the brain is most active. In many cases, they do not think about the consequences but base their decisions on recent data or "gut instinct." Therefore, in their brains, signals travel from the eyes to the visual area of the left side of the brain and are recognized as a pattern.

Due to lack of complete awareness of the meaning of these patterns, the signal will be transmitted to higher levels of the visual cortex and will pass to the amygdala and the right side of the brain in search for answers. Because there are no previous charts to compare with, the signal will bring affective dissonance, which means that the trader might feel bad with physical manifestations of fear and anxiety. Within the body, the signals will continue moving back and forth, leading to a lot of questioning, second-guessing, thinking, and a horde of internal battles.

From this back and forth movements, a state of confusion emerges that might make the trader take any of these two actions. The trader might execute the trade or back out of the trade entirely to alleviate his anxiety. Whichever step he takes will only lead to more stress and more internal confusions. Even if the trade goes in his favor, there may be more losses in the future, because his decisions are not based on fact but rather his attempts to alleviate anxiety or fear. This is the reason why novice traders make a lot of mistakes which results in severe losses for them. They can only understand recent or surface trends.

Experts

With the experts, the reflective part of the brain is used. However, it looks like the reflexive because it has been developed and engineered to recognize a lot of patterns[xxix]. With those stored patterns, he can analyze and emerge with reliable deductions. So, when he sees patterns, his brain processes quickly because he has seen it before, so there is no dissonance as a result of receiving the signal. When the signal enters the brain through the eyes, it goes up to the visual area of the neocortex as a pattern and then to the hippocampus, which recognizes the pattern. From there, it moves to the amygdala and then to the right sections of the brain, where the limbic structures bring about a good feeling because there is recognition. Fear or anxiety, in this case, is lesser than that witnessed by the inexperienced trader. These signals will travel to the prefrontal thinking areas, where there it will be analyzed, and then it will move to the motor area of the brain and be executed as trade.

Training

Looking at the differences between the brain of the novice and expert, you should realize that training your brain is essential. When you train your brain for trading, you are influencing your trading strategies and decision making. Training the brain helps you build your resilience in different situations[xxx]. It would also increase your capacity to change, organize, progress, concentrate, and move more towards trading excellence. You can only train the brain by diligent, intense, and committed practice while going through market cycles for many years. As a result, you bring more harmony between the two sections of your brain, process patterns accurately and instantly. Ultimately, you make less inaccurate decisions and a lot more profits.

Chapter 4

TRADING REQUIRES CALCULATED RISKS

The power of taking risks lies in the fact that it is a standpoint to access more significant opportunities. There is hardly any successful person who achieved what they did without taking risks. There are a lot of traders who are afraid to take risks. They do not want to take risks because they fear that they may lose money. Indeed, when it comes to trading, you can lose significant amounts of money by taking the wrong risk. There are principles you need to master to manage the risks effectively. Every good trading plan must make provisions for managing risks. It is one of the most crucial aspects of trading. Without taking conscious steps to manage the risks in trading, there might be adverse consequences.

While learning, your general goal would be to minimize your losses until you can understand many more things about the market from a strategic and analytical perspective. If you are an experienced trader, you may want to develop a realistic risk management strategy that would help you grow admirably. No matter your level in the scheme of things, applying the following rules is paramount to success[xxxi].

Determine Your Trading Size
- Position Sizing

Your level of risk tolerance should influence the capital you risk. Ideally, you make those decisions with a clear focus. The capital varies from trader to trader, so you must trade with a size that will allow you to make rational decisions. No adequate capital size exists. Trading with too much capital often results from many emotional influences fuelled by a lack of discipline.

Some traders choose their position size by trying to envisage their profits. If they do not predict a win, they trade too little. If they have high hopes of winning (especially after a winning streak), they place a higher trading size. Although the end goal is to make money, making your assessments on how profitable the trade will potentially be is dangerous. You must ensure that you analyze your trading size logically. Most trading errors can be minimized by sizing down.

Aside from determining your position size by your emotional abilities, ensure you determine the size of the position you will be taking in that particular trade when the opportunity comes. This is an effective risk management strategy and can be performed in different ways. For instance, you can determine the risks you will take on in any given position by comparing the total value of your portfolio. It's also an excellent idea to trade in relative terms than absolutes. This involves sticking within a position size but varying it from time to time.

Drawdowns, Frequencies and Trading Style

So, you have a good idea what the rules are, when calculating risks, you may wonder how to determine the amount of risk in your trade. Initially, we talked about position sizing. Now, we want to consider other factors that can influence your trading size. First, you must consider that you will have lots of drawdowns (we will discuss this in a later chapter). So, your ideal position size should be determined with this fact in mind. It's possible to have problematic drawdowns where losses pile up ten or more in a row. You always want to account for this and calculate your "max pain" if all of your stops hit because the general market isn't cooperating. Your position size can also be affected by how frequently you trade. If you trade less frequently and hold trades for several weeks, you have more risk per trade since you need to have wider stops on longer timeframe charts.

- Pay Attention to The Loss, Not the Wins

You must focus on the process and not the money. Therefore, you need to find trades that offer an asymmetrical risk profile. I understand that we all don't want to lose money, but drawdowns are natural to this game of uncertainty. So, rather than get stuck on the high win ratio, look for win rates that are reasonably lower with an unbalanced risk outlook.

- Envisage the number of drawdowns you can take

If a trade isn't going well, you can also consider when you want to pull out of the trade. This involves what Brett Steenbarger calls "accepting the obvious." Since drawdowns are part of the trade, you want to set a limit to how much you can take. Taking that step back is always better than seeking alternative trades that can "fix" the problem.

- Leverage with Caution

When you add a highly leveraged trading position to an underfunded trading account, it can be beneficial. However, you must tread with caution. Leverage and margins are best used by people who understand their capabilities and limitations. When one has no idea how to make leverage work, it can lead to more losses quickly[xxxii].

- Make Diligent Hard Stops

Discipline and patience are vital for the long game.

Therefore, you need to implement strategies that will apply those in your trading. Using a hard stop is prudent. A hard stop is a stop-loss you can enter into the trading system. The opposite of it is a soft stop, where you have a predetermined level your mind cooked up that should be triggered. By using a hard stop, you stop before your emotions spiral out of control. Secondly, you don't need to watch the screen judiciously. Unforeseen events are a part of the game. If you are a veteran trader than you can use soft stops but it is highly recommended that as a novice trader who still has yet to master their own emotions, you let the stop do the work for you instead of requiring you to intervene again one more time to make a decision.

Do you want to trade successfully? Then you must realize that managing your risks is essential. However, remember that you can't avoid risks in trading. So, you must prepare yourself mentally, logically, and financially for the risks involved. An excellent risk management strategy is always the best way to manage the probability of uncertainty.

Chapter 5

TRADING IN PROBABILITIES

There are lots of uncertainties to deal with, but the good thing is that most of the time, you can measure those uncertainties and figure how much you can handle. This does not depend only on your risk management strategy but understanding the laws of probability trading. The probability of trading is the likelihood of a trade being successful[xxxiii].

As we have discussed in earlier sections of this book, your mind can and will play games with you from time to time, especially when you are assessing how successful your trades might be. These games will also depend on your psychological state at the time, the level of recent winnings, and external events unrelated to trading.

Generally, before any trade, most traders can maintain an objective view, especially after analyzing the different parameters and coming up with a logical conclusion of something that should work for them. After placing the trade, their minds might trick them into believing that they have more chance of winning than what reality holds. In an earlier section, we described this as confirmation bias, and it is a huge problem.

In trading, you can't hold onto the belief that things are 100% true until proven otherwise. Trading does not work in that direction. The likelihood of the success of any trade is between 40% - 60%, and it can be influenced by the timing, trading style, and market conditions.

Avoid the Flaws of Instinctual Trading

You need to understand that you can be successful with 40% of your trades and make a lot of money, if only you manage risk correctly[xxxiv].

As emotional beings, it can be challenging to understand this theory; the brain is not naturally wired to accept that there might be up to 60% more losses. But you must realize that you can also have up to 80% wins and still lose money with poor risk management. It isn't necessarily about the percentage of wins vs losses but how short you cut your losses and how long you let your winners run.

Furthermore, you must avoid making overestimations on losing a trade. Such behavior has caused a lot of people to take the route of under trading. This is because losing affects people more than winning. To make sure you aren't over trading or under trading, avoid the following mindsets:

- The Gamblers Mentality

In this case, there is no adoption of the 100% mentality but a mindset that I can win or lose by 50%. So, the trader believes that he can lose or win at random and would most likely depend on instinct to place the trade than analyze the underlying parameters. Some traders also adopt this mentality after a series of gains or losses.

So, how do you make the probabilities work in your favor?

Avoid the mentality of being right or wrong, focus instead

on achieving the little realistic goals you put in place. Be prepared as much as possible before you place any trade. According to Nial Fuller[xxxv], your 'battle plan' is vital to this war. However, never allow yourself to get too confident. Whenever you plan, reassess what you want to go with by asking yourself these questions:

- What beliefs are there in my system?
- Am I trading on beliefs or facts?
- Why am I following this strategy?
- Can they be wrong? How wrong can they get?
- Are they unsupportive or supportive?

When you use these questions time and time again to reevaluate your trading strategy, you can adapt it to the changing knowledge, eliminate all possible errors in judgment, and increase your chances of winning over time.

Secondly, adopt the mathematical approach but keep things simple. What separates the inexperienced trader from the professional trader is the ability think in probabilities. In simpler terms, you need to get comfortable with uncertainty.

Chapter 6

CONSTRUCTIVE SELF-DEVELOPMENT

We have discussed the brain and the emotional roller coaster that can impede upon trading decisions. Controlling your emotions is crucial, but it goes beyond managing stress or using the right trading tactics. You also have to develop your mindset in ways that will affect your approach to life generally. In this chapter, we will look at some of these crucial aspects that will transform your trading for the better.

What Kind of Trader Are You?

You must have a general idea of what makes you tick. You need to look inwards and fill in the gaps. The kind of trader you are will affect everything you do. It will help you figure out your position sizing, your trading style, the level of risks you can take, how you want to prepare your portfolio, and much more. Get a journal and run this evaluation[xxxvi][xxxvii].

- In a few sentences, describe yourself?
- When you trade, how do you talk to yourself? Are you frustrated or angry, defeated, or negative? Do you focus your self-talk on the market? How much do you focus on you? Is your self-talk destructive or constructive?
- What do you do in your free time?
- Why do you trade?
- Do you consider yourself a passive or active trader?
- Are you a dreamer or do you like making routines?
- Can you identify your specific edges or your weaknesses?
- Do you thrive in uniformity or emotional upheaval?

There are many more questions you can ask yourself, but these areas provide the foundation. Pick up that journal and document how you react to events, your key strengths, and weaknesses. Understanding yourself can help you get a better handle of your emotions. It can also help you figure out the kind of emotional judgments you might likely make in specific scenarios. The goal is to know yourself inside and out and to come to the realization that all trading errors are solved internally and not externally.

A Word on Consistency

Consistency is an important skill you need in trading[xxxviii]. It refers to repetitive or constant use of a specific set of trading principals by an individual. You can never understate its importance to your overall trading. Developing a consistent trading strategy and sticking to it through thick and thin will help you make sensible decisions over time. When you are consistent in your approach, you can avoid overtrading and can sustain appropriate risk management.

Practicing consistency means following a thorough analytical plan, having a trading strategy, avoiding under trading and over trading, enacting proper risk management rules, and tracking and reviewing your trading plan over time[xxxix]. Consistency also involves making sure that your trading plan is detailed. Just as there are aspects of trading you cannot control, there are many other aspects that rely on your choice. So, use them to your advantage by planning. There are lots of ways to execute on defined opportunities but be consistent about how you execute or use those opportunities.

Another important thing you must do is to ensure consistency by journaling your affairs. When you journal your wins, losses, and other factors over time, you will be able to make better decisions. When you are consistent, you can avoid the influences of emotions. This is because you are not pushed into taking irregular or irrational decisions which can lead to inconsistent results over time. It will also help you build the right edge in the market because you are sticking to the methods, the trading size, the entries, and exits that you are familiar with.

A Confident Outlook
- While you make decisions about your trading, what happens within you?
- Do indecisions or emotional upheavals strike you because you have no idea if you are on the wrong path?

If yes, you need to develop your confidence. When you are confident about you, you can follow things through. You can make smart decisions and be prepared to accept when your predictions don't come through. Having that confidence, that 'can-do' attitude, will help you become focused on your goals. In the face of obstacles, you will be able to face them efficiently.

Confidence will also help you pick the trading style that suits your personality. The crowd of emotions of the general markets won't influence your decisions. Through confidence, you can accelerate your learning curve.

On the other hand, lack of confidence is destructive. Without confidence, you might doubt those carefully laid out trading plans you have. Without confidence, you might be prone to flip in all directions, searching for what you can find right before your eyes. Build a positive perspective, and you can overcome hurdles, obstacles, and make more in the long run.

Focus on the Process

While you learn how to analyze, understand the market, and set your trading plan, you also need a goal. Naturally, you might want to set goals such as making profits, but that also means that your emotional state will be subject to the ups and downs in the market. Remember you are trading in uncertainties, so such plans are dangerous.

Focus on the process of learning[xl]. Focus on how you stick with your trading plan, how you execute trades and stay within the limits of your risk management plan. Focus on fulfilling those goals – they are realistic, precise, and will ultimately bring profits to you naturally. You should also be very specific about those goals. Outline your daily routine, as well. By daily routine, I mean outlining what you do from the moment you wake till the time you go back to bed at night. You also need to construct a precise, repetitive process for how you analyze the market.

Developing Resilience

You also need to build resilience. Resilience is the ability to recover quickly from challenges. Because trading has lots of drawdowns, resilience is an in-demand skill. Bear in mind that successes do not push you to higher levels of resilience[xli]. You learn to be resilient by having setbacks and growing from them. Resilience helps you understand and acknowledge the importance of failure in success. According to Brett Steenbarger, "You become successful when you fail fast and fail often[xlii]."

Think of it in terms of trying to lose weight. You don't stop because your muscles hurt or because after a few weeks you can't see any change in your weight. You keep your eyes on the prize and by doing so; get better, stronger, and healthier.

There is no growth without failure; failure can serve as the right motivation, a source of learning, and inspiration. When you become resilient, you gain the willpower to continue bouncing back no matter how much you are pushed to the ground. You keep failing and conquering, building on your resources but not quitting.

To build resilience, you need to become spiritually and emotionally fit[xliii]. You need to create caring and supportive relationships within and outside your family. You also need to have the capacity to make realistic plans and follow them through. You need to build skills in problem solving and communication. So, go out there and make new connections. Join different groups, support others, and be supported. Avoid looking at crisis as an overwhelming feat you can't overcome. You should also learn to accept that change, whether for good or bad is a part of life. Search for new opportunities to discover you and take decisive decisions, no matter the situation.

When you are resilient, every day looks like an opportunity to learn. Each drawdown would be an opportunity to learn, even more, drawing on your positive psychological reserves until you can turn that failure into success.

Chapter 7

STRESS MANAGEMENT TO EXERT CONTROL

Putting all of your money into a savings account and leaving it there for twenty, thirty or fifty years requires no risky choices, triggers no stress responses, but also fails to bring you the types of returns that can genuinely make a difference in your life. Trading introduces a much higher degree of risk, even when you follow all the best practices and strategies.

Sometimes, you will lose money, make bad trades, and find yourself in a problematic situation that includes more risk and psychological distress than you intended.

As a trader, you have lots of decisions to make and fast. Every decision comes with lots of uncertainties and probabilities that it can go haywire no matter how much you analyzed.

There's no secret that trading is a stressful business. 2 out of 5 traders deal with extreme stress every day[xliv]. The tension is so high that over 75 percent of traders quit after the first two years. According to Business Insider[xlv], it's the second most stressful job after investment banking.

Stress can negatively influence your performance to a significant level. Don't get sucked into the myth that with the more money you make, the less stress you have. You must realize that stress can make a lot of people make too many errors in judgment.

The stress we feel has a lot to do with our hormones. When we have more testosterone as a result of trading, it also enhances the stress hormone, cortisol. Cortisol is sensitive to situations of uncertainty, novelty, and uncontrollability[xlvi]. With high cortisol levels, traders can have clouded judgments and anxiety, which causes them to make erratic decisions.

Understanding how to handle this type of stress is one of the most important aspects of maintaining control over your entire trading strategy. As long as you do not allow the volatility of the market to create a harsh and uncontrollable emotional response, you will avoid making knee-jerk decisions that can make a bad situation much worse.

To some, the following suggestions for stress management and emotional control may feel excessively new age. However, as you will see, each has a strong scientific backing that clearly shows its benefit to your life. According to research[xlvii], successful traders acknowledge the stress and take steps to manage it. A different study[xlviii] points out that stress resistance is one of the top five attributes of a successful trader. They work well for any stress experienced with your career, relationships, or financial situation. Before we discuss the ways and manner you should manage stress, let's look at some symptoms of stress.

According to Admiral Market[xlix], here are signs to look out for:
- Sweating
- Nail-biting
- Breathing difficulty

- Palpitations
- Trembling hands
- Overreacting
- Loss of appetite or overeating
- Restlessness
- Tense muscles
- Loss of sleep
- Depression

Always remember that the more stress you have, the higher the risk of making a lot of trading errors. When these errors are made, one loss can lead to yet another loss. However, also note that stress in small amounts can be beneficial to your performance. But you must manage it, to keep it at that limited stance. Here are some ways you can manage stress effectively:

Practice Meditation

Meditation is a practice of calming your mind and emotions to be mindful of yourself and your surroundings[1]. It is a way to relax, reset your mind, improve your mood, and reduce stress.

The benefits of meditation when it comes to financial management and trading are considerable. Since you have learned that calm or a less emotional mind makes smarter trading decisions, you may like to adopt the practice of sitting quietly and relaxing for a few minutes before you start your day. You can also do it at other times when you particularly feel stressed or overwhelmed.

Consider the following tips for effective meditation practice:

- Choose a comfortable location and position
- Close your eyes if you prefer and pay attention to your breathing
- Practice mindfulness, which means you become aware of yourself and everything around you in a calm and nonjudgmental manner
- Observe your thoughts. Don't be your thoughts
- Guided meditation, audio, and video may help you achieve more benefits by making it easier to sit still in the beginning

Positive Thought Reframing

Controlling what you think and managing emotional responses allow you to take control of how you feel. The process of reframing your thoughts goes beyond positive thinking or using affirmations. It is a way to promote optimism without excessive enthusiasm or glee. After all, balanced emotions and a firm grasp on psychological effects help you make better decisions about your financial future.

How do you reframe your thoughts? The process itself seems quite simple. Do not be used to negativity, else you will find reframing difficult. In essence, when you think something negative, you change it around to be a positive statement instead. The positive affirmation does not change the situation. Instead, it merely changes how you think about the situation. It allows you to retain a greater sense of control over potentially harmful reactions.

Some examples of positive thought reframing:

If a trade does not go as well as expected, and you lose a chunk of money, you may automatically think something like, "I have such horrible luck with tech stocks." This type of negativity is, first of all, unhelpful because it could stop you from investing in tech in the future, and also, is probably not true. If you do not get a high rate of return on tech investments, perhaps you need to research more and open your journal to ignite and jot down new ideas.

Reframe this thought for increased positivity by saying something like, "I can put more time into studying the tech industry." Negativity and feeling sorry for yourself will not get you to where you want and is unproductive.

If you buy in when the stock price is already going up past your pivot, an emotional response that focuses on negativity may sound like, "I always miss the best time to buy." Even if you have never purchased a single share at the absolute bottom of its pullback, a statement like this creates an excessively emotional response that cannot help you. It may even push your mind to focus on buying future stocks too early in hopes of getting that elusive low price. Try reframing this thought with a statement like, "I always follow my rules and wait for confirmation."

Restructure Time and Activities

Some say that a change is as good as rest. If you find yourself overwrought or overworked, you increase the chance of a psychological response to everything you attempt to do. You may become vulnerable and give in to your emotions rather than using cognitive power to make decisions.

Getting stuck in a rut affects some people negatively because their accepted and preferred practices begin to breakdown due to complacency. While you created a plan and rules for your trading, you are more likely to stop focusing on them or following them exactly if they drift out of focus. This happens in many different aspects of your life. For example, if you want to curtail your financial expenditure, you must forget about excesses that aren't profitable. Another great scenario is someone trying to lose weight. You may stick to a diet very firmly at the beginning, but soon, you grab an extra cookie or a soda instead of water at the vending machine. Your plan to approach financial investments and trading may start to experience the same type of problem if you do not shake things up once in a while. Lets look at how we can shake things up.

Micro-breaks and Mini-vacations

This stress-relieving technique can involve meditation, and it is the idea behind restructuring your time and activities. Micro-breaks and mini-vacations[li] allow you to reset your mind so it can function better afterward. The vast majorities of people do not start work at 8 AM and continue till 5 PM without any breaks or diversions. You can talk to the person next to you for a few minutes, get up and walk to the water cooler, sit back and sip your coffee, or any number of other non-work activities. All of these things are micro-breaks that are essential for your cognitive function to continue. Especially as a novice trader it is easy to become glued to the screen and feel the need to watch every tick. You must learn to detach yourself from the market so that the relationship is healthy.

Mini-vacations are the grander version of micro-breaks that give your brain an extra chance to release stress. These do not include flying to Hawaii for the weekend unless you are fortunate. Most mini-vacations include day trips, or merely taking a mental health day from work or other responsibilities.

You may wonder if you have time to take a day off of your research and trading activities. Now that you understand how important it is to manage your stress levels and avoid the emotional responses that come with market volatility, you may wonder if you can afford not to.

"The techniques I developed for studying turbulence, like weather, also apply to the stock market." – Benoit Mandelbrot, mathematician, economist, and inventor of fractals.

The classic stock market investment adage of "Buy low and sell high," or my favorite "Buy high and sell higher" represents the fundamental truth of becoming one of the less than 5% who earned a considerable amount of money in the market — knowledge matters. An understanding of stock pricing and business practices can help fuel the possibility of success. However, what differentiates winners from losers is their psychological control and emotional restraint when it comes to reacting to fluctuations and volatility.

Historical stock market crashes demonstrate how emotion fuels the numbers on a grand scale. For your investment portfolio, the same thing happens when you lose sight of your particular goals. In the constant struggle between fear and optimism, your mind must act as a mediator to ensure smart actions in both the short and long terms.

Forget your impression of harried day traders with migraines and stress ulcers desperately trying to squeeze an extra penny from every share they buy. Forget the trap of confusion and strain that leaves many people hiring expensive financial managers to choose stocks and funds for them. Forget feeling like every decision you make or fail to make will result in abject loss or ultimate wins. Understanding and managing psychological aspects of the stock market can allow you to increase your returns without succumbing to extreme stress.

Most of all, you can use the information and techniques written here to facilitate a comfortable and sure type of growth that benefits you in the future without robbing you of comfort. Anyone can learn how to invest successfully in the stock market and avoid the roller coaster of both emotional response and profitability.

Create Your Own Stock Strategy

You must realize that studying stock charts and deep research matters if you want to buy the right shares and make a good return on your investment. It represents the type of information gathering any trainer has to do unless they pay a fee to an assistant to do it for them.

However, beyond the statistics comes the psychology of stock trading. You have to understand that emotions fuel buying and selling decisions. It, in turn, can affect the market at large, but always affects how your particular investments do.

These automatic and physiological responses to price fluctuations happen whether you want them to or not. Nevertheless, you have the power to create a strategy to manage them and avoid the knee-jerk trading responses that too many other people give in to.

A Very Basic Look at Stock Market Advice

While there is a multitude of tips and tricks to boost your profits on Wall Street, most of them come down to the following few ideas.[lii]

- Invest only in what you are comfortable losing
- Focus on the overall picture instead of particulars
- Diversify your investments and stock purchases
- Think long-term to manage volatility
- Foster a sense of calm and objectivity

The majority of people who have studied trading have learned these steps already. They are part of the logical process necessary to reduce risk and increase the possibility of returns. How do you create a winning strategy in the face of all these psychological issues that influence trading at large?

Choose Your Overall Goal Wisely

If I ask you, "Why do you want to get involved with trading?" One of your first answers will undoubtedly have something to do with money. After all, why would you purchase shares from a particular company or fund if you did not want that investment to grow? Money is the number one goal of any investing strategy.

Money itself means very little.[liii] Instead, what you want out of trading includes comfort for you and your family, a secure retirement, a better future for your children, and an end to worry and concern. Not surprisingly, what you want out of the stock market is fueled by as much emotion as your decisions about what to invest in, how much, and when.

Of course, some people think money is the most important thing. They want to acquire more of it because they believe it gives them power over people who have less. Unfortunately, in this world, that attitude is quite prevalent and accurate. Still, the real desire relies on the emotion of fear that they will not measure up to personal or societal expectations.

What is your goal? Whether you want to pay for your child's university degree or want to wear $5,000 shoes to impress other people, recognize that your goals are emotional rather than practical. The sooner you accept that you are an emotional being who must use appropriate measures to overcome this, the sooner you will be able to make intelligent trades and satisfy your goals in general.

What should your goal be? It is not the purpose of this book to make judgment calls about what you want in life. However, to understand and apply the psychology of trading and improve your own returns, the goal should be trading mastery and skill acquisition.

As psychologists, investment analysts, and attorneys know, money is one of the most significant sources of stress in the entire world. If you attempt to make decisions based on money alone, you allow the emotional response to dictate your actions. Understanding this is very different than overcoming it.

"FINANCIAL FREEDOM IS FREEDOM FROM FEAR."– ROBERT KIYOSAKI, AUTHOR OF *RICH DAD, POOR DAD*

Chapter 8

MEDITATION AND MINDFUL TRADING

As discussed in an earlier chapter, meditation can make a difference in your trading. Many trading meditation strategies have their roots in religion, but overtime, they have been proven to work effectively. However, you may wonder why you need to meditate. It sure sounds like a religious mantra that's not going to work. But there are scientific studies where meditation has been more effective than traditional medicine[liv].

Meditation is perfect for you. Trading can be very stressful to the body. It might cause us to enter the fight or flight response often, which produces a lot of hormones and alters our mental state, which can cause limited mental performance. According to a recent study by Fadel Zeidan, mindfulness meditation showed a significant drop in anxiety levels of participants by altering brain activities in the ventromedial prefrontal cortex (which controls worries) along with the ACC (anterior cingulate cortex) that regulates emotion and thinking. Through meditation, those areas of the brain can be stimulated to reduce anxiety and stress.

Apart from altering anxiety, meditation can also prevent mental decline. As we age, our brain's volume and weight decrease with a significant loss in grey matter. Soon, our functional mental abilities decline as well. In a study by Dr. Florian Kurth at the UCLA, meditation limits the loss of the grey matter, which is an incredible phenomenon. If you want to keep your brain fresh for a very long time, the best path you should take is to meditate.

When you trade better as a result of these strategies, your quality of life improves, and ultimately you can reach fulfillment in both your trading and personal life. In another study on Meditation by Professor Eileen Luders at UCLA, she discovered that people who meditate have stronger brain region interactions. This allows the brain to send signals swiftly across the brain regions[lv]. The study also found that white matter fibers were denser, insulated, and more abundant throughout the brain among the long-term meditators. Through this study, it was widely acknowledged that meditation could re-write the brain and change its anatomy.

Meditation can equally increase your awareness of your actions and reactions to the happenings in your life. With that heightened level of consciousness, you can control overexcitement, lower stress, and even limit conflicting internal dialogues. Meditation can help you appreciate the moment and develop patience which is vital for long term success[lvi]. Meditation induces calmness and takes away anxiety. With mediation, you build and maintain a centered perspective, and find a balance between your emotional and cognitive responses to an event.

Do you still wonder why you need meditation to develop the successful trader's mindset? Ponder on the words of Chris Capre[lvii].

"You don't use a specific compartmentalized section for trading. We didn't evolve to be traders sitting in front of a computer for our survival, so we must use the neurons and skills from all portions of our brains. Our brain is an interconnected whole which is made up of our memory, the mindset of abundance, fear, greed, family, memory, confidence, and a lot more and we use all of these areas together to make those trading decisions."

What is Mindful Meditation?

Mindfulness meditation is a form of meditation that delivers more. Mindfulness is taking action to understand your entire being in a holistic wonder. It is a way of everyday things we often overlook in an entirely different dimension with awe and reverence[lviii]. Mindfulness is not only a journey but a lifestyle. It is more than an attempt to control your emotions. Mindfulness provides a holistic view of reality. It will help traders recognize that a lot of things the mind says aren't always in sync with reality.

Mindfulness offers a platform to observe our thoughts, feelings, and bring our mind to the present so we can pay attention to the things that matter. When you practice mindful trading, it will not only affect your trading but will change the way you eat, walk, talk, compete, play, work, and explore. Mindfulness works because it is intentional and deliberate. With Mindfulness, you will not only view trades on the bases of heuristics and cognitive biases but be able to see every other thing that makes each decision-making process critical.

The words of Gary Dayton can best explain everything in simplest terms;

"Mindfulness is a quality of consciousness. You can see it as paying attention in a particular way: on purpose, in the present moment, and nonjudgmentally. It is also a state of mind; you can develop through persistence to enhance concentration and attention. Mindfulness allows you to separate yourself from your thoughts and feelings, and it further helps you stay focused on the present moment rather than drift off into the past or future."

From these words, you can see specific instructions. First, Mindfulness is a deliberate or conscious act. So, it means you must learn how to do it. Secondly, it is not a skill you perfect in a day, but over time through consistency, you will improve your ability to pay attention to the present.

Practice Mindful Trading

Scientific studies have explained how beneficial mindfulness is to our mental health. So, what is the next step? How does mindfulness impact on our trading? First, you need to understand the principles of mindful trading. You need mindfulness every step of the way.

When preparing for your trading session, what is the framework you lean on? How do you harness new information? How do you evaluate the information you have? A single market has unlimited ways to access information. You also need to be alert for those uncontrollable market instances that will influence your trading decisions.

Beyond observing and making sure that your trading preparations are thorough, you also need to follow the trade with a wholesome perspective. When you take the holistic view of your trading, it would be easier to concentrate on information without bias or distractions. Our minds are prone to wander, so this step is essential. Mindfulness provides adequate support to shut out all those interruptions and distractions to a significant level.

Lastly, practicing mindfulness in the heat of the action is also crucial. It will help you handle your emotions, so they don't cause you to make errors that might lead to losses. Mindfulness centers on a calm, detached, and expansive view that can help you interpret the market much more accurately. Navigating the markets becomes much clearer when you practice mindfulness successfully.

A Basic Form of Mindfulness

There are different kinds of mindfulness trading practices, but here are the most popular and necessary forms you can try. However, remember that you must practice over time to become excellent at self-control. Long term meditators have better self-control and have a more positively modified brain structure[lix].

Step 1 – Posture

Take a seat on a comfortable chair and maintain a healthy posture. Relax and align your backbone as though there is a string attached to the top of your head and pulling upwards. Place your feet flat on the floor and your arms on your lap or the arms of the chair.

Step 2 – Deep breathing

Now, take a deep breath and hold it for a few seconds, then exhale gently. As you repeat this step, close your eyes to increase awareness. Take another deep breath, hold, and exhale. Take a third deep breathe and focus on how it fills your body; you don't have to control it, watch and then slowly exhale.

Step 3 – Pay attention

Next, take a deep breath, this time; follow it with your mind. Focus on how it moves from your nostrils to your mouth, brain, and other areas in your body. Notice the sensations that surround your breathing. Watch your breath and do nothing else.

Step 4 – Bring your attention back

As you focus on your breath, your mind may wander. Once you are aware of it, don't immediately try to bring your mind back. Notice what you were thinking, and how your body reacts to it. When you become aware, gently bring your attention back to the breath. Time and time again, your mind will wander because the brain thinks it is better to concentrate on actual thoughts. Each time your mind wanders, accept those thoughts, don't be upset or alarmed. It is a natural part of the process. All you need to do is gain awareness, receive it, then gently bring your mind back to the breath.

Tips to Get Started with Mindful Practice

Apart from the primary form of mindfulness, you need to explore other areas as well. You can begin by designating a time and space for it. It will help you eliminate external interruptions. You don't need an elaborate space. A simple chair should be enough. You can also begin by scheduling your mindfulness session for 5 minutes. Over time, you can move upward to 10 minutes or more.

Some people find the morning hours excellent for mindfulness; others prefer noon or nighttime. Find your preference and stick with it. You can also practice twice or more a day. The basic form of mindfulness meditation in this book might not work for everyone. You should also research other types of mindfulness, which can work for you. You can walk mindfully, listen mindfully, focus on breathing, use a mantra, and much more. However, here are some more tips you can add for better results[lx]:

1 – Write down your emotional state at the closing of the trade

How did you feel at the close of the trade? Were you excited, irritated, or depressed? As a beginner to mindfulness practice, you might not be very aware of it. So, you need to pick up a journal and write your thoughts in a narrative at that moment. When you write, you will recognize the extreme thoughts that may have crossed your mind, even when the trade went in your favor. With that awareness, you can prevent those emotions in the next trade. Over time, you will be able to pick those adverse reactions that can be dangerous to your decision making.

2 - Use workout sessions

Regular workout sessions are vital. They can help you manage stress and must be used in connection with mindfulness for better results. You don't have to go to the gym daily or exercise for long hours. Do whatever you are comfortable with but make sure it is regular.

3 – Watch your nutrition

You should also practice mindful eating. These include

mindful or deliberate consciousness of what you eat, why you eat that, and how you even prepare your meals. When you watch what you eat, you will understand your essential eating habits, reactions, and make an effort to eat healthy meals.

As you practice mindfulness, you will begin to observe your thoughts and feelings. You will no longer be a slave to them which will bring you one step closer to the true reality. Always remember that mindfulness will not only help you pay attention to the trade; it will help you in other areas of your life.

Chapter 9

TEN TIPS TO GET YOU STARTED TOWARDS TRADING CORRECTLY

Managing psychological and emotional responses gives you the best platform for making smart trading decisions. The first step to creating any change in your life or your strategies to accomplish any goal is to accept that most of the process lies in your mind.

With the demonstrations and explanations found in the earlier parts of this book, you should recognize that the stock market rises and falls based on the emotional responses of all the people buying and selling. Also, you begin to understand how fear and greed, or optimism fuels your actions and reactions to the changes that continuously occur in your financial portfolio.

Understanding does not directly correlate to the practical application of smart management techniques. You can know something is right without understanding how to address the problem. The following ten tips give you functional changes to make in your life to overcome the psychological hold your brain has on the trading process.

1. Educate Yourself or Find an Educated Helper

This tip is both the most obvious and, perhaps, the most important. Between the internet and the wide variety of books out there, you can find any information you are searching for about how the stock market works, statistics surrounding the S&P 500, best investment practices and more.

You have two options to make the trading process more comfortable. First, you can spend money hiring a respected professional to handle all your trades for you. Secondly, you can spend time learning what you need to know to feel confident in your trading decisions. The first option negates almost any intellectual or emotional interaction with the process entirely. The second will require the rest of the nine tips, or at least some of them, to temper your expectations, minimize reaction with impact, and reduce the stress level that the entire trading process brings.

"It is true that millions come easier to a trader after he knows how to trade than hundreds did in the days of his ignorance."
- Jesse Livermore

The quote above by the great Livermore is one of my favorites. I am a firm believer that the stock market is the ultimate wealth-building machine. The learning curve is one of the most prolonged and most demoralizing experiences you will ever encounter. But being able to reap profits out of the market consistently is one of the most rewarding experiences you can come across.

2. Figure out Your Ultimate Goals

If you believe your overall goal is money, you have already missed the point of this psychological guide to trading. Remember that emotions fuel every decision based on wants and perceived needs. You do not need money. You want the comfort, peace of mind, or power it gives you. One of the most common reasons to consider investing with the stock market is to ensure long-term financial growth to fund a comfortable retirement. It remains an intrinsic part of every single person's life experience.

Identifying your goal allows you to attach a meaningful emotion to the entire process of trading. However, beware of the possibility of transcending practicality and focusing only on the dreams of a high-priced supercar, or the type of attention you would get if you had more money. Also, keep in mind that essential goals may trigger a sense of loss aversion that gets in the way of appropriate amounts of risk during your trading activities.

Ideally, make sure that your goals are intelligent, measurable, and practical. It will allow you to keep track of your forward progress and make wiser decisions based on statistics and data, rather than psychological responses.

"If a man knows not which port he sails, no wind is favorable." – Seneca

For me, I trade for income to live and pursue my passions like traveling. Outside of money, I trade for the sheer competition it brings. Show me a professional trader, and I'll show you someone who has control over themselves, extreme discipline and doesn't succumb to the never-ending rambling of the mind.

3. Stick to a Plan and Rules That Makes Sense

Put rules into place that protects you from making quick and potentially stupid decisions you will regret down the road. If X happens, then you do Y. If X does not arrive, you respond with Z.

Of course, because the markets change so much, and you cannot definitively put every occurrence into a neat box, some flexibility must exist within your list of rules. However, making an actual plan that you agree is nonnegotiable gives you a measure of control that you would not have if you operated based on psychological responses and the natural emotions you feel when you make money or lose it.

If you face every situation without a plan, you may only have a small amount of time to study the possibilities appropriately and make a decision. Rushing invites emotions to take hold because it feels like the chance of missing out is much higher than if you sit back and see what happens next. The latter option frequently makes a big difference in the long run.

All of the work is done before you enter the trade. Once you enter a trade, there is no more reason to guess or waste any more mental capital on that position. You must follow your rules systematically. Remember we want to detach from the market.

4. Maintain Individuality in the Face of Herd Mentality

If all your friends jumped off a bridge into the river, would you follow them? This classic parental question seeks to find out how susceptible you are to the herd mentality. This concept goes far beyond childhood peer pressure. The stock market itself is a force primarily concerned with the attitudes and ideas of a large mass of investors. If you go along for the ride with whatever everyone else is doing, you will not be able to make intelligent decisions about what truly makes sense.

It speaks directly to the fear and greed cycle that creates market volatility and drastic situations like stock market crashes. One technique that I use to gauge market sentiment is the Put/Call Ratio or PC Ratio for short. This number is found by dividing the total number of puts by the total number of calls daily.

When the PC reading is high (above 1.0), the market tends to be in panic mode. The majority of participants are fearful and looking down, so what tends to happen? The market forms a short-term bottom and moves up while everyone is apprehensive and looking down.

When the PC reading is low (below .85), the market tends to be in greedy mode. Investors are looking up and buying strength in the market. What happens when the crowd is greedy and looking up? You guessed it! The market tends to form a short-term top and pull back.

5. Protect Yourself From 'Ooh, Something Shiny!' Decisions

Day traders operate on the thin edge of the investment knife. Part of their modus operandi is to quickly identify shiny trades that indicate the possibility of quick profits. The vast majority of people who invest in the stock market are not day traders, and these rapid and informed decisions are not necessary for long-term growth. If you spot something at the right time and buy shares quickly, of course, you can realize a high profit. However, trying to do that regularly leads to extreme stress and a higher possibility of making emotional decisions rather than informed ones.

How do you protect yourself from pursuing the next best thing? First, if you created a plan and rules as described in Step #3, you already have protections in place against heading off in a new and dangerous direction. If something shiny attracts you, form a comparison in your mind to a glass ornament. Yes, it looks quite enticing and valuable. However, those qualities also contribute to its delicacy and fragility. If you cannot back up a stock idea with research, knowledge, and a proper risk management strategy, you run the risk of making a wrong decision.

Like I mentioned previously, most of your work is done before you enter the trade. If you never planned for a trade, then do not take it. There will always be another set up coming around, or the same one will come back to get you. Do not succumb to the pressure of FOMO.

6. Think and Research Before You Act

Knowledge destroys fear. The more you know about a particular industry, the track record of a specific opportunity, or the general trends of the overall stock market, the better equipped you are to handle its volatility. Understanding how dangerous it is to make decisions based on emotion should lead you to develop a continuous habit of educating yourself.

Take time every day or week to study these things and learn how everything works in the trading world. The simple habit of using your intellect to fill up the financial aspect of your life will help drive out emotional responses more fully. You only have so much brainpower to commit to any particular interest. Always remind yourself that the practical study, application of learning and brainpower, but not your gut, should fuel trades.

Your research should include scanning the chart for institutional accumulation and a favorable risk to reward. Are you a breakout trader? A pullback trader? Whatever you look for, make sure a prospect has the set up you are looking for with the proper risk to trade it.

7. Take Time to Imagine "Winning"

Everything we do starts from the brain[lxi]. It is essential to always focus your mind on the positive. Do not communicate any unfavorable energy around you before taking a trade. Remember it isn't about any one trade but a series of trades overtime. When you have a proper plan despite taking a loss you will be able to avoid the emotional responses that come with it because you understand that you are still winning over a series of trades. Always calculate your risk and expect that your stops will hit but revert back to your plan and acknowledge to continue winning you don't need this trade to work.

8. Stop Analysis Paralysis

This clever phrase refers to the practice of researching or preparing excessively before taking any action. Several steps outlined in this book already tell you to gather information and make a plan before you start trading. Of course, you should always know what you are doing before you do it. However, analysis paralysis is a fear reaction that stops you from moving forward with your plan.[lxii] It severely dampens your ability to make informed decisions about purchasing shares or selling them when appropriate.

Simple problems and solutions present themselves to handle this trading block:

- Are you confused by outside input? Turn it off or block them out.
- Are you succumbing to fear that you may make a mistake? Take a risk while understanding you always have the opportunity to make different choices in the future.
- Is excessive information blocking your brain? Go back to your plan for research and investing decisions.

I trade price and volume. I keep my charts empty, and I focus on what is important to me. I ignore any outside input and follow my plan. The more indicators that you have, the more conflicting signals you are going to get, which will paralyze you when it is time to execute. Any hesitation in your execution is proof that you are yet to truly accept and prepare for the random outcomes of each of your trades.

9. Cultivate Smart Responses to Loss

Whether you experienced loss aversion before you even take any action or succumb to despair and depression, if you end up losing some money in one of your trades, you need to figure out a better response so you can move forward.[lxiii] Fear makes sense from your nervous system's perspective. If you lose something, even money, you have a sense of danger and concern that you will not have enough or enjoy the same levels of comfort as you did in the past.

That fear or despair can quickly turn to even worse problems if you allow it to take control and push you into trades that you have not researched thoroughly.

Always remember that "High emotion does not create the best atmosphere for smart choices."

How do you cultivate a more intelligent and less emotional response to loss? First, you need to assign less fear to the concept of failure. Some people find it beneficial to avoid the word failure at all cost because it carries a lot of very negative connotations. Instead of seeing any loss so seriously, frame it within the bounds of your entire financial situation. If you are an intelligent stock market investor, you do not put all your eggs in one basket. Therefore, other funds may temper the distinct loss you have with just one trade.

10. Keep Long-term Records and Journals

One of the best ways to mitigate your psychological or emotional response to stock market trading is to keep track of everything over the entire length of your trading history. Plenty of financial software programs and apps allow you to do this easily. They create attractive graphs that show you clearly whether your money is growing or shrinking.

Even if one particular stock goes down, seeing a visual representation of growth allows you to stay in a more positive mindset. It helps you avoid the negative responses to fear and despair but also protects you against excessive optimism fueling uninformed purchase or sale decisions. The big picture always tells a more accurate and practical story than an individual trade does.

Keep a journal for every single trade you place, your entry, your exit, and even leave room to write down your thought process at the time you put on the trade. There is a lot of valuable data to be captured that numbers alone won't portray. Make yourself accountable for every single decision that you make, and you will be able to see where your losses are arising from clearly.

Chapter 10

HANDLING A TRADE DRAWDOWN

No bigger emotional event exists in trading than dealing with drawdowns. A drawdown is that valley between new equity highs on your equity curves[lxiv]. In the short term, it is that period of loss. No one likes having a drawdown, but if you want to avoid them altogether, then you need to get out of the trading path. There's no such thing as trading without drawdowns – they are natural.

Some people also believe that drawdowns are rare events that happen once or twice in a year or two. But the reality is that a lot of traders spend more than 75% of their time in a drawdown, even when it looks like they are making a profit.

The only reason, they aren't aware of these drawdowns sometimes is because there are two distinct types. First, there is a normal drawdown. This kind results from the flow of your trading, and, in most cases, you can control those losses. Prepare for it and be more ready to evaluate the reasons behind them.

The second is the problematic scenario – that's when losses begin to pile up, ultimately leading to distress. Sometimes they happen because of biases, errors, or other poor trading behavior. In many of these occasions, more problems might arise because the distress can be so overwhelming that the trader might make more mistakes, damaging themselves mentally and financially.

So, what do you about these drawdowns? For starters, you have to learn to live through them. It means you must prepare mentally for them. If you are going to spend more than a quarter of your trading time in these areas, you have to become aware of them, study them, and live through it. You need to understand that as long as trading is a function of probabilities, then drawdowns are probable events as well. It can be a terrible experience, but it's a normal part of it. However, bear in mind that your strategies for handling drawdowns might not necessarily be the same.

If you are handling a normal drawdown, then it might be that you are not trading efficiently or maybe your trading strategy isn't cooperating with the market at the time. So, it might mean that you need to check for minor errors and reevaluate the market conditions.

On the other hand, if you are handling a problematic drawdown, you might consider stopping for some time.

Compounding the situation by looking for alternatives or adopting the disastrous gambling mentality of finding that one trade that can win back all is not ideal. Taking a little time off doesn't solve the problem, but it provides adequate time to regroup and strategize. When you go out, you may have difficulty stepping away, but when you finally do, you will feel immense relief. Experts consider doing this recuperation for a few days. To further explain how to handle drawdowns, there are a few more tips you can use.

1. **Accept That There is No Way to Avoid These Risks**

As said earlier, you need to develop the mentality that drawdowns are inevitable. Expect that a new drawdown can even arise in the future, or that an average drawdown can spiral out of control.

Drawdowns, whether regular or problematic, can also be caused by market conditions. The market is in constant flux[lxv] because the financial, political, and economic environments change as well. So, when the price shifts, which it does consistently, it results in different motions that can go either way. It is so important to have a trading plan that you stick to so that you can learn to recognize when drawdowns are from execution error or when it is the general market environment that has changed. Many traders trade through environments that are uncooperative with their strategy because they believe the problem is within their execution and this is where the most account damage takes place because you should have been patient.

2. Change Your Perspective

Think about other areas in your life and measure your blessings. Forget about reveling in sorrow or trying to believe that you have failed in some way. Avoid equating failure with your trading losses. The only thing that has changed is the lesser funds in your trading account balance. Your unique skills are still intact, and you can climb out of the drawdown sometime in the future but not today. Look for more ways to lighten the emotional stress. Talk a walk, meditate, or practice mindfulness. On a general note, look at the brighter side of things.

3. Avoid Increasing Your Position Size

A common mistake some traders make when facing a drawdown is to believe that they can get out of the drawdown by increasing their position size. As Ed Seykota[lxvi] would always say, **"Trying to trade a losing streak is emotionally wrecking. Trying to play "catch up" is lethal."**

Avoid both by eliminating the mentality that increasing the position size can be your way out. That's a gambler's mentality, but not the mindset of an expert trader who wants to make more profits than losses. This might look contradictory, but it is a given fact. You can't know when the losing streak will end – the normal drawdown can always spiral out of proportion – even if your trading strategy was "foolproof." Impulsive trading can cause more errors which can be fatal.

4. Avoid Making Adjustments to Your Trading Method

Instead of making changes in your trading style, think in this way "the market conditions are not favorable for my trading style now; I can always try again with the same trading style, sometime in the near future." Consistency pays off in the long run. Believe in your strengths, your abilities, and your trading plan. When you change your system because of a drawdown which those changes can go in different directions, it automatically resets your learning curve, putting you back at stage one of your trading style.

5. Measure Your Drawdowns

Although you shouldn't change your trading style, you need to analyze what went wrong within that time. Ask yourself these questions:
- Did I execute flawlessly?
- Did I stick with my trading plan?
- Did I violate any trading rules?

With these three questions, you can figure out the errors made, if any or, maybe evaluate the conditions of the market and take a more proactive step that wouldn't include trying to fix it.

6. Think About the Long-Term Goal

Look at the goals you want to achieve in the future. Use positive affirmations to remind yourself of the reasons why you are trading or even doing business in general. There's still a long way off, and those goals can be fulfilled sometime in the future. You are only having a bad week/quarter but sticking to your long-term trading plan is crucial. If you haven't created a long- term trading plan, you must do so now.

Having a consistent trading strategy helps you always make sensible decisions. It provides a clear path to stick to what you are already doing when the goings are tough. It's easier to take a proactive step in the same direction as before when you already know where you are heading to[lxvii]. However, you must always make sure you set process goals instead of monetary goals. When you set monetary goals, you end up with unnecessary build-ups of pressure. So, you need more effective goals that focus on your trading process.

7. Analyze the Past

While checking out the factors that lead to the drawdown you are facing now, look at similar drawdowns you have faced in the past. When you look at those events from the past, you will realize that you may have them, but it went unnoticed because it wasn't so bad. When you analyze the past, it ensures that you are following a very consistent path in your trading. Analyzing the past will also help you become aware of any action you have taken that stepped away from your comprehensive trading plan.

8. Learn to Step Away from the Screen

Before you analyze anything or figure out what went wrong, take a walk. If you try differently to talk to yourself during those initial moments, when your performance anxiety is relatively high, you might inaccurately process the data. Bear in mind that although the patterns and data are all in front of you, your brain is responsible for what you deduce from that data. Right now, it is in a flight or fight response stage, so, there will be too many emotional responses clouding that single logical action. It's far better to step away from the screen so that when you return; you can refocus and accurately take your next action than act on your fears which will compound the already stressful situation[lxviii].

Conclusion

As you flip or scroll the pages of this book, there must have been internal struggles as you uncover new factors, new strengths that can make the difference to your trading. You must realize that beyond your proper methods, instincts, and systems, everything else depends on the state of your emotions.

Emotions drive trading, so, when one has an avalanche of emotions, that individual will likely make a myriad of decisions that can hurt rather than sustain the process.

Throughout this book, you must have realized one important detail – You alone are the key to your successes. What you do with the skills you have, your emotions, your perception, and functions will impact your trading. No matter how influential your mentor is to you, they shouldn't impact your decisions in the way you can.

So, the choice is yours, you can decide to stick to a few rules, build a strategy, and make a few profits or you can choose to dive deeper. When you journey on the path of self-discovery, you can tap into enormous wells of resources which can ultimately lead to better decisions, fewer drawdowns, and more profits. You need to build your resilience in the ever-changing markets. Trust me; when you develop your cognitive, emotional, and social strengths, you will be able to see the market on a whole different level.

Trading is not about a set of routines but a repetitive process orientation. Trading is about research, generating ideas, structuring your trades, managing your risks, managing your performance, and of course, managing yourself. So, becoming the expert or achieving elite performance depends on how far you go to deepen your strengths. You succeed when you turn all of these fascinating practices into habits. Take full responsibility for everything you do on this journey, and you can drive better performance. Develop yourself, your perception, and strengths, and you will transform every part of your trading and your life as well.

About the Author

My name is Nick Schmidt. Back in the beginning of 2017, I met my current mentor, Ross Haber who is a former Portfolio Manager for William O'Neil + Co. He helped take my trading to the next level and really stressed the importance of ignoring all the noise, including the news and focusing only on price action.

When I am not trading, I am spending time with my husky Brody, or traveling the world. Traveling the world, and trading allows me to pick up and go as I please. Not because it is easy to make money but because all I need is my laptop and an internet connection.

I was first introduced to meditation and the art of

mindfulness about three years ago. This has immensely improved my trading and overall quality of life. I struggled for years as a trader, looking for strategies that didn't exist. I went through substantial financial & emotional setbacks on the journey to profitability. My constant failures made me question my future as a trader. As I became serious about my trading through self-reflection, I realized that the path to consistency had nothing to do with a strategy and everything to do with my mindset. Incorporating this into my trading has helped me to steadily develop the mindset and mental skills that would lead me to my path of consistency.

NICK SCHMIDT

[i] https://www.tradeciety.com/24-statistics-why-most-traders-lose-money/
[ii] https://phys.org/news/2015-12-stock-investor-emotions-fuel-frenzy.html
[iii] https://phys.org/tags/emotional+states/
[iv] https://www.kiplinger.com/article/investing/T031-C032-S014-psychology-of-stock-market-and-investment-decision.html
[v] https://smallbusiness.chron.com/emotional-theory-stock-market-1815.html
[vi] https://www.investopedia.com/articles/investing/012116/warren-buffett-be-fearful-when-others-are-greedy.asp
[vii] https://www.1stglobal.com/blog/how-your-emotions-affect-stock-market
[viii] https://economictimes.indiatimes.com/topic/Reuters
[ix] https://economictimes.indiatimes.com/markets/stocks/news/how-fear-destroys-your-wealth-when-the-market-is-in-turmoil/articleshow/66474519.cms?from=mdr
[x] https://en.wikipedia.org/wiki/Greed_and_fear
[xi] https://medium.com/swlh/market-crash-psychology-d22e3456bf33
[xii] https://www.1stglobal.com/blog/how-your-emotions-affect-stock-market
[xiii] https://www.marketwatch.com/story/heres-how-stock-market-investors-can-control-their-emotions-2018-07-31
[xiv] Gary Dayton, (2015) Trade Mindfully. John Wiley & Sons, Inc. Hoboken, New Jersey
[xv] https://www.investopedia.com/articles/trading/02/110502.asp
[xvi] www.brettsteenbarger.com
[xvii] https://www.psychologytoday.com/us/blog/the-wide-wide-world-psychology/201301/the-biological-basis-the-thrill-victory
[xviii] https://www.psychologytoday.com/us/blog/the-power-the-status-quo/201905/what-does-loss-aversion-mean-investors
[xix] https://onlinelibrary.wiley.com/doi/abs/10.1002/jcpy.1047
[xx] Gary Dayton, (2015) Trade Mindfully, John Wiley & Sons Inc., Hoboken, New Jersey
[xxi] Gary Dayton, (2015) Trade Mindfully, John Wiley & Sons Inc., Hoboken, New Jersey
[xxii] https://en.wikipedia.org/wiki/Base_rate_fallacy
[xxiii] https://www.investopedia.com/terms/b/base-rate-fallacy.asp
[xxiv] https://sharpbrains.com/blog/2008/06/05/your-brain-on-trading-101/
[xxv] https://sharpbrains.com/blog/2008/06/05/your-brain-on-trading-101/
[xxvi] https://www.netpicks.com/gap-trade-planning-execution/
[xxvii] Brett N. Steen Barger (2015) Trading Psychology 2.0, John Wiley & Sons, Hoboken, New Jersey.
[xxviii] https://www.amazon.com/gp/product/0743276698/ref=s9_simh_gw_p14_d6_i1
[xxix] https://sharpbrains.com/blog/2008/06/05/your-brain-on-trading-101/
[xxx] http://traderfeed.blogspot.com/2016/08/how-can-we-train-our-brains-for-trading.html
[xxxi] https://www.dailyfx.com/forex/education/trading_tips/daily_trading_lesson/2018/03/22/Becoming-a-Better-Trader-Principles-of-Risk-Management-Video-PRtech.html
[xxxii] https://www.forextraders.com/forex-education/forex-money-management/leverage-and-its-risks/
[xxxiii] https://excellenceassured.com/8225/law-probability-trading
[xxxiv] https://excellenceassured.com/8225/law-probability-trading
[xxxv] https://www.learntotradethemarket.com/forex-currency-trading-blog/trading-probabilities-in-your-favor
[xxxvi] https://tharptradertest.com/default.aspx?question=1
[xxxvii] http://www.brettsteenbarger.com/

[xxxviii] https://www.dailyfx.com/forex/education/trading_tips/daily_trading_lesson/2019/04/10/how-to-trade-consistently.html
[xxxix] https://www.dailyfx.com/forex/education/trading_tips/daily_trading_lesson/2019/04/10/how-to-trade-consistently.html
[xl] https://dailypriceaction.com/blog/forex-trading-goals/
[xli] https://www.forbes.com/sites/brettsteenbarger/2015/03/16/turning-setbacks-into-successes/#51a174d7f51c
[xlii] https://www.forbes.com/sites/brettsteenbarger/2015/03/16/turning-setbacks-into-successes/#51a174d7f51c
[xliii] https://www.apa.org/helpcenter/road-resilience
[xliv] https://www.metlife.co.uk/who-we-are/media-centre/2017/february/demanding-bosses-turn-up-the-pressure-on-city-stress-/
[xlv] http://www.businessinsider.com/the-most-stressful-jobs-on-wall-street-2014-1
[xlvi] http://www.pnas.org/content/105/16/6167
[xlvii] https://bit.ly/2llvgbT
[xlviii] https://bit.ly/2lUidE4
[xlix] https://admiralmarkets.com/analytics/traders-blog/5-crucial-tips-for-overcoming-stress-when-trading
[l] https://www.healthline.com/nutrition/12-benefits-of-meditation
[li] https://www.bbc.com/worklife/article/20190312-the-tiny-breaks-that-ease-your-body-and-reboot-your-brain
[lii] https://www.thestreet.com/investing/how-to-make-money-in-stocks-14846188
[liii] http://tradingcomposure.com/money-goal/
[liv] https://www.tradingminds.net/post/why-meditation-effective-path-to-trading-success
[lv] Gary Dayton (2015) Trade mindfully; Achieve optimum trading performance with mindfulness and cutting edge psychology, John Wiley & Sons. Hoboken, New Jersey
[lvi] https://www.fxstreet.com/education/the-benefits-of-mindful-meditation-for-your-trading-201903190523

[lvii] https://2ndskiesforex.com/trading-strategies/forex-strategies/developing-a-successful-forex-trading-mindset-pt-2/

[lviii] https://www.fxstreet.com/education/the-benefits-of-mindful-meditation-for-your-trading-201903190523

[lix] Gary Dayton (2015) Trade mindfully, achieves optimum trading performance with mindfulness and cutting-edge psychology, John Wiley & Sons. Hoboken, New Jersey
[lx] https://www.warriortrading.com/5-tips-for-exercising-mindfulness/
[lxi] https://kids.frontiersin.org/article/10.3389/frym.2018.00069
[lxii] https://www.learntotradethemarket.com/forex-articles/cure-traders-analysis-paralysis
[lxiii] https://www.mytradersstateofmind.com/learning-to-deal-with-failure-differently---building-a-winning-trading-psychology.html
[lxiv] https://www.netpicks.com/5-things-need-live-drawdowns/
[lxv] https://optimusfutures.com/tradeblog/archives/why-do-drawdowns-exist-and-how-to-deal-with-them-efficiently
[lxvi] https://optimusfutures.com/tradeblog/archives/why-do-drawdowns-exist-and-how-to-deal-with-them-efficiently
[lxvii] https://www.dailyfx.com/forex/education/trading_tips/daily_trading_lesson/2019/04/10/how-to-trade-consistently.html
[lxviii] www.brettsteenbarger.com

Printed in Great Britain
by Amazon